CW00326496

ESSENTIAL
Chicken

p

Contents

Introduction

Once a luxury appreciated only by the affluent, chicken is now a worldwide family favourite. In fact, today chicken is the most popular meal for Sunday lunch in Britain, New England, Italy and France alike. Like Henry IV of France, who enjoyed chicken so much that he insisted all of his subjects must be able to afford to eat roast chicken for Sunday lunch, most would agree that it is delicious.

Chicken is a versatile, tasty and reasonably priced white meat which lends itself well to many recipes because of its subtle flavour. It can be cooked with herbs, spices, fruit and vegetables, and suits both sweet and savoury flavours.

Chicken also has a low fat content. For those who are conscious of their calorie and cholesterol intake, it is the perfect choice. To obtain a moist succulent meat without sacrificing your healthy eating regime, cook the chicken with the skin on and then remove it just before serving. However, if you want to reduce fat even further simply remove the skin from the chicken and cook by poaching, grilling (broiling), roasting or stir-frying. Chicken is also an excellent source of protein and contains valuable minerals, such as potassium, phosphorus and some of the B vitamins.

The range of chicken available today is wide. If you want to try something different try baby chicken or poulet de Bresse. Baby chicken, also known as poussin or Cornish game, tastes best when stuffed or marinated. One whole bird is usually needed for each person.

Poulet de Bresse chickens are reared in the Burgundy region of France and are fed on natural, high-quality food in free-range conditions. These chickens although expensive, are considered to be superior in quality.

When buying fresh chicken always check the sell-by date and ensure that the chicken is chilled. Choose a chicken with no dark patches, which is free of feathers and smells clean and fresh. Fresh chicken should feel soft and flexible to the touch and give slightly when pressed.

The recipes in this book are gathered from a variety of cuisines and suggest various cooking techniques.Choose from soups, snacks, barbecues and grills, pasta, Indian, Chinese and hot-and-spicy chicken dishes. All are guaranteed to be mouth-watering and flavoursome.

Chicken & Asparagus Soup

Serves 4

INGREDIENTS

225 g/8 oz fresh asparagus
850 ml/1¹/2 pints/3³/4 cups
    fresh chicken stock
150 ml/5 fl oz/²/3 cup dry
    white wine

1 sprig each fresh parsley, dill
    and tarragon
1 garlic clove
60 g/2 oz/¹/3 cup vermicelli
    rice noodles

350 g/12 oz lean cooked
    chicken, finely shredded
salt and white pepper
1 small leek

1 Wash the asparagus and trim away the woody ends. Cut each spear into pieces 4 cm/1½ inches long.

2 Pour the stock and wine into a large saucepan and bring to the boil.

3 Wash the herbs and tie them with clean string. Peel the garlic clove and add, with the herbs, to the saucepan together with the asparagus and noodles. Cover and simmer for 5 minutes.

4 Stir in the chicken and plenty of seasoning. Simmer gently for a further 3– 4 minutes or until heated through.

5 Trim the leek, slice it down the centre and wash under running water to remove any dirt. Shake dry and shred finely.

6 Remove the herbs and garlic and discard.

7 Ladle the soup into warm bowls, sprinkle with shredded leek and serve at once.

VARIATION

You can use any of your favourite herbs in this recipe, but choose those with a subtle flavour so that they do not overpower the asparagus. Small, tender asparagus spears give the best results and flavour.

COOK'S TIP

Rice noodles contain no fat and are an ideal substitute for egg noodles.

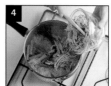

Clear Chicken & Egg Soup

Serves 4

INGREDIENTS

1 tsp salt	1 leek, sliced	1 tbsp dry sherry
1 tbsp rice wine vinegar	125 g/4¹/2 oz broccoli florets	dash of chilli sauce
4 eggs	125 g/4¹/2 oz/1 cup shredded	chilli powder, to garnish
850 ml/1¹/2 pints/3³/4 cups	cooked chicken	
chicken stock	2 open-cap mushrooms, sliced	

1 Bring a large saucepan of water to the boil and add the salt and rice wine vinegar. Reduce the heat so that it is just simmering and carefully break the eggs into the water, one at a time. Poach the eggs for 1 minute. Remove the poached eggs with a slotted spoon and set aside.

2 Bring the stock to the boil in a separate pan and add the leek, broccoli, chicken, mushrooms and sherry and season with chilli sauce to taste. Cook for 10–15 minutes.

3 Add the poached eggs to the soup and cook for a further 2 minutes. Carefully transfer the soup and poached eggs to 4 individual soup bowls. Dust with a little chilli powder to garnish and serve immediately.

COOK'S TIP

You could use 4 dried Chinese mushrooms, rehydrated according to the packet instructions, instead of the open-cap mushrooms, if you prefer.

VARIATION

You could substitute 125 g/4¹/2 oz fresh or canned crabmeat or the same quantity of fresh or frozen cooked prawns (shrimp) for the chicken, if desired.

Curried Chicken & Sweetcorn (Corn) Soup

Serves 4

INGREDIENTS

175 g/6 oz can sweetcorn
(corn), drained
850 ml/1¹/₂ pints/3³/₄ cups
chicken stock
350 g/12 oz cooked, lean
chicken, cut into strips

16 baby corn cobs
1 tsp Chinese curry powder
1-cm/¹/₂-inch piece fresh root
ginger (ginger root), grated

3 tbsp light soy sauce
2 tbsp chopped chives

1 Place the canned sweetcorn (corn) in a food processor, together with 150 ml/¹/₄ pint/²/₃ cup of the chicken stock and process until the mixture forms a smooth purée.

2 Pass the sweetcorn purée through a fine sieve, pressing with the back of a spoon to remove any husks.

3 Pour the remaining chicken stock into a large pan and add the strips of cooked chicken. Stir in the sweetcorn (corn) purée.

4 Add the baby corn cobs and bring the soup to the boil. Boil the soup for 10 minutes.

5 Add the curry powder, ginger and soy sauce and cook for 10–15 minutes. Stir in the chives.

6 Transfer the soup to warm bowls and serve.

COOK'S TIP

Prepare the soup up to 24 hours in advance without adding the chicken, let cool, cover and store in the refrigerator. Add the chicken and heat the soup through thoroughly before serving.

Chick Pea (Garbanzo Bean) & Chicken Soup

Serves 4

INGREDIENTS

25 g/1 oz/2 tbsp butter
3 spring onions (scallions),
 chopped
2 garlic cloves, crushed
1 fresh marjoram sprig,
 finely chopped

350 g/12 oz boned chicken
 breasts, diced
1.2 litres/2 pints/5 cups
 chicken stock
350 g/12 oz can chick peas
 (garbanzo beans), drained
1 bouquet garni

1 red (bell) pepper, diced
1 green (bell) pepper, diced
115 g/4 oz/1 cup small dried
 pasta shapes, such as
 elbow macaroni
salt and white pepper
croûtons, to serve

1 Melt the butter in a large saucepan. Add the spring onions (scallions), garlic, sprig of fresh marjoram and the diced chicken and cook, stirring frequently, over a medium heat for 5 minutes.

2 Add the chicken stock, chick peas (garbanzo beans) and bouquet garni to the pan and season with salt and white pepper.

3 Bring the soup to the boil, lower the heat and then simmer gently for about 2 hours.

4 Add the diced (bell) peppers and pasta to the pan, then simmer for a further 20 minutes.

5 Transfer the soup to a warm tureen. To serve, ladle the soup into individual serving bowls and serve immediately, garnished with the croûtons.

COOK'S TIP

If preferred, use dried chick peas (garbanzo beans). Cover with cold water and set aside to soak for 5–8 hours. Drain and add the peas to the soup, according to the recipe, and allow an additional 30 minutes– 1 hour cooking time.

Sage Chicken & Rice

Serves 4

INGREDIENTS

1 large onion, chopped
1 garlic clove, crushed
2 sticks celery, sliced
2 carrots, diced
2 sprigs fresh sage
300 ml/^{1}/$_2$ pint/1^1/$_4$ cups chicken stock
350 g/12 oz boneless, skinless chicken breasts

225 g/8 oz/1^1/$_3$ cups mixed brown and wild rice
400 g/14 oz can chopped tomatoes
dash of Tabasco sauce
2 medium courgettes (zucchini), trimmed and thinly sliced
100 g/3^1/$_2$ oz lean ham, diced

salt and pepper
fresh sage, to garnish

TO SERVE:
salad leaves
crusty bread

1 Place the onion, garlic, celery, carrots and sprigs of fresh sage in a large saucepan and pour in the chicken stock. Bring to the boil, cover the pan and simmer for 5 minutes.

2 Cut the chicken into 2.5 cm/1 inch cubes and stir into the pan with the vegetables. Cover the pan and continue to cook for a further 5 minutes.

3 Stir in the rice and chopped tomatoes. Add a dash of Tabasco sauce to taste and season well. Bring to the boil, cover and simmer for 25 minutes.

4 Stir in the sliced courgettes (zucchini) and diced ham and continue to cook, uncovered, for a further 10 minutes, stirring occasionally, until the rice is just tender.

5 Remove and discard the sprigs of sage. Garnish with a few sage leaves and serve with a fresh salad and fresh crusty bread.

COOK'S TIP

If you do not have fresh sage, use 1 tsp of dried sage in step 1.

Chilli Chicken & Sweetcorn Meatballs

Serves 4

INGREDIENTS

450 g/1 lb lean chicken,
  minced (ground)
4 spring onions (scallions),
  trimmed and finely
  chopped
1 small red chilli, deseeded
  and finely chopped
2.5 cm/1 inch piece root
  (fresh) ginger, finely
  chopped
100 g/3¹/₂ oz can sweetcorn
  (no added sugar or salt),
  drained

salt and white pepper
boiled jasmine rice, to serve

TO GARNISH:
spring onions (scallions) and
  red (bell) pepper, chopped

SAUCE:
150 ml/5 fl oz/²/₃ cup fresh
  chicken stock
100 g/3¹/₂ oz cubed pineapple
  in natural juice, drained,
  with 4 tbsp reserved juice

1 medium carrot, cut into thin
  strips
1 small red (bell) pepper,
  deseeded and diced
1 small green (bell) pepper,
  deseeded and diced
1 tbsp light soy sauce
2 tbsp rice vinegar
1 tbsp caster (superfine) sugar
1 tbsp tomato purée (paste)
2 tsp cornflour (cornstarch)
  mixed to a paste with 4 tsp
  cold water

1 To make the meatballs, place the chicken in a bowl and add the spring onions (scallion), chilli, ginger, seasoning and sweetcorn. Mix together.

2 Divide the mixture into 16 portions and form each into a ball. Bring a pan of water to the boil.

Arrange the meatballs on a sheet of baking parchment in a steamer or large sieve (strainer), place over the water, cover and steam for 10–12 minutes.

3 To make the sauce, pour the stock and pineapple juice into a pan and bring to the boil. Add

the carrot, (bell) peppers and pineapple, cover and simmer for 5 minutes. Stir in the other ingredients and heat through, stirring, until thickened. Season.

4 Drain the meatballs and transfer to a serving plate. Garnish and serve with rice and the sauce.

Crispy-Topped Stuffed Chicken

Serves 4

INGREDIENTS

4 boneless chicken breasts,
about150 g/5^{1}/$_2$ oz each,
skinned
4 sprigs fresh tarragon
^{1}/$_2$ small orange (bell) pepper,
deseeded and sliced
1^{1}/$_2$ small green (bell) pepper,
deseeded and sliced

15 g/^{1}/$_2$ oz wholemeal
breadcrumbs
1 tbsp sesame seeds
4 tbsp lemon juice
1 small red (bell) pepper,
halved and deseeded
200 g/7 oz can chopped
tomatoes

1 small red chilli, deseeded
and chopped
^{1}/$_4$ tsp celery salt
salt and pepper
fresh tarragon, to garnish

1 Preheat the oven to 200°C/400°F/Gas Mark 6. Slit the chicken breasts with a sharp knife to create a pocket in each. Season inside each pocket.

2 Place a sprig of tarragon and a few slices of orange and green (bell) peppers in each pocket. Place the chicken breasts on a baking sheet (cookie sheet) and sprinkle over the breadcrumbs and sesame seeds.

3 Spoon 1 tbsp lemon juice over each chicken breast and bake in the oven for 35–40 minutes until the chicken is cooked through.

4 Preheat the grill (broiler) to hot. Arrange the red (bell) pepper halves, skin side up, on the rack and cook for 5–6 minutes until the skin blisters. Cool for 10 minutes; peel off the skins.

5 Put the red (bell) pepper in a blender,

add the tomatoes, chilli and celery salt and process for a few seconds. Season to taste. Alternatively, finely chop the red (bell) pepper and press through a sieve with the tomatoes and chilli.

6 When the chicken is cooked, heat the sauce, spoon a little on to a warm plate and arrange a chicken breast in the centre. Garnish with tarragon and serve.

Chicken with a Curried Yogurt Crust

Serves 4

INGREDIENTS
---

1 garlic clove, crushed

2.5 cm/1 inch piece root
(fresh) ginger, finely
chopped

1 fresh green chilli, deseeded
and finely chopped

6 tbsp low-fat natural
(unsweetened) yogurt

1 tbsp tomato purée (paste)

1 tsp ground turmeric

1 tsp garam masala

1 tbsp lime juice

4 boneless, skinless chicken
breasts, each 125 g/4^1/2 oz

salt and pepper

wedges of lime or lemon, to
serve

RELISH:

4 medium tomatoes

^{1}/4 cucumber

1 small red onion

2 tbsp fresh coriander
(cilantro), chopped

1 Preheat the oven to
190°C/375°F/Gas
Mark 5. In a small bowl
mix together the garlic,
ginger, chilli, yogurt,
tomato purée (paste),
turmeric, garam masala,
lime juice and seasoning.

2 Wash and pat dry the
chicken breasts and
place them on a baking
sheet (cookie sheet). Brush
or spread the spicy yogurt
mix over the chicken and

bake in the oven for 30–35
minutes until the meat is
tender and cooked through.

3 Meanwhile, make the
relish. Finely chop the
tomatoes, cucumber and
onion and mix together
with the coriander
(cilantro). Season, cover
and chill until required.

4 Drain the cooked
chicken on absorbent
kitchen paper and serve hot

with the relish. Or, allow to
cool, chill for at least 1
hour and serve sliced as
part of a salad.

VARIATION

*The spicy yogurt coating
would work just as well if
spread on a chunky white
fish, such as cod fillet. The
cooking time should be
reduced to 15–20 minutes.*

Chicken & Plum Casserole

Serves 4

INGREDIENTS

2 rashers lean back bacon,
    rinds removed, trimmed
    and chopped
1 tbsp sunflower oil
450 g/1 lb skinless, boneless
    chicken thighs, cut into
    4 equal strips
1 garlic clove, crushed

175 g/6 oz shallots, halved
225 g/8 oz plums, halved or
    quartered (if large) and
    stoned
1 tbsp light muscovado sugar
150 ml/5 fl oz/²/₃ cup dry
    sherry
2 tbsp plum sauce

450 ml/16 fl oz/2 cups fresh
    chicken stock
2 tsp cornflour (cornstarch)
    mixed with 4 tsp cold
    water
2 tbsp flat-leaf parsley,
    chopped, to garnish
crusty bread, to serve

---

1 In a large, non-stick frying pan (skillet), dry fry the bacon for 2–3 minutes until the juices run out. Remove the bacon from the pan with a slotted spoon, set aside and keep warm until required.

2 In the same frying pan (skillet), heat the oil and fry the chicken with the garlic and shallots for 4–5 minutes, stirring occasionally, until well browned all over.

3 Return the bacon to the frying pan (skillet) and stir in the plums, sugar, sherry, plum sauce and stock. Bring to the boil and simmer for 20 minutes until the plums have softened and the chicken is cooked through.

4 Add the cornflour (cornstarch) mixture to the frying pan (skillet) and cook, stirring, for a further 2–3 minutes until thickened.

5 Spoon the casserole on to warm serving plates and garnish with chopped parsley. Serve with chunks of bread to mop up the fruity gravy.

VARIATION

Chunks of lean turkey or pork would also go well with this combination of flavours. The cooking time will remain the same.

Chicken Pasta Bake
with Fennel & Raisins

Serves 4

INGREDIENTS

2 bulbs fennel
2 medium red onions, shredded
1 tbsp lemon juice
125 g/4^1/2 oz button
    mushrooms
1 tbsp olive oil
225 g/8 oz penne (quills)

60 g/2 oz/^{1}/3 cup raisins
225 g/8 oz lean, boneless
    cooked chicken, skinned
    and shredded
375 g/13 oz low-fat soft
    cheese with garlic and
    herbs

125 g/4^1/2 oz low-fat
    Mozzarella cheese, thinly
    sliced
2 tbsp Parmesan cheese, grated
salt and pepper

1 Preheat the oven to 200°C/400°F/Gas Mark 6. Trim the fennel, reserving the green fronds for garnishing, and slice the bulbs thinly. Coat the onions in the lemon juice. Quarter the mushrooms.

2 Heat the oil in a large frying pan (skillet) and fry the fennel, onion and mushrooms for 4–5 minutes, stirring, until just softened. Season and

transfer the vegetable mixture to a large bowl.

3 Bring a pan of lightly salted water to the boil and cook the penne (quills) according to the instructions on the packet until 'al dente' (just cooked). Drain and mix the pasta with the vegetables.

4 Stir the raisins and chicken into the pasta mixture. Soften the soft

cheese by beating it, then mix into the pasta and chicken – the heat from the pasta should make the cheese melt slightly.

5 Put the mixture into an ovenproof dish and transfer to a baking sheet (cookie sheet). Arrange the Mozzarella on top and sprinkle with the Parmesan. Bake for 20–25 minutes until golden. Garnish with fennel fronds and serve.

Chicken Tikka

Serves 6

INGREDIENTS

1 tsp fresh ginger root, finely chopped	1 tsp salt	3 tbsp oil
1 tsp fresh garlic, crushed	2 tbsp lemon juice	
1/2 tsp ground coriander	a few drops of red food colouring (optional)	TO GARNISH:
1/2 tsp ground cumin	1 tbsp tomato purée (paste)	6 lettuce leaves
1 tsp chilli powder	1.5 kg/3 lb 5 oz chicken breast	1 lemon, cut into wedges
3 tbsp yogurt	1 onion, sliced	

1 Blend together the ginger, garlic, ground coriander, ground cumin and chilli powder in a large mixing bowl.

2 Add the yogurt, salt, lemon juice, red food colouring (if using) and the tomato purée (paste) to the spice mixture.

3 Using a sharp knife, cut the chicken into pieces. Add the chicken to the spice mixture and toss to coat well. Leave to marinate for 3 hours, or preferably overnight.

4 Arrange the onion in the bottom of a heatproof dish. Carefully drizzle half of the oil over the onions.

5 Arrange the marinated chicken pieces on top of the onions and cook them under a pre-heated grill (broiler), turning each piece once and basting with the remaining oil, for 25–30 minutes.

6 Serve the chicken tikka on a bed of lettuce and garnish with the lemon wedges.

COOK'S TIP

Chicken Tikka can be served with Naan Breads, Raita and Mango Chutney or as a starter.

Chicken Tossed in Black Pepper

Serves 4-6

INGREDIENTS

8 chicken thighs
1 tsp fresh ginger root, finely
    chopped
1 tsp fresh garlic, crushed
1 tsp salt
1 1/2 tsp pepper
150 ml/1/4 pint/2/3 cup oil

1 green (bell) pepper, roughly
    sliced
150 ml/1/4 pint/2/3 cup water
2 tbsp lemon juice

FRIED CORN & PEAS:
50 g/2 oz unsalted butter
200 g/8 oz frozen sweetcorn

200 g/8 oz frozen peas
1/2 tsp salt
1/2 tsp chilli powder
1 tbsp lemon juice
fresh coriander (cilantro)
    leaves, to garnish

1 Using a sharp knife, bone the chicken thighs, if you prefer.

2 Combine the ginger, garlic, salt and coarsely ground black pepper together in a mixing bowl.

3 Add the chicken pieces to the black pepper mixture and set aside.

4 Heat the oil in a large pan. Add the chicken and fry for 10 minutes.

5 Reduce the heat and add the green (bell) pepper and the water to the pan. Leave the mixture to simmer for 10 minutes, then sprinkle over the lemon juice.

6 Meanwhile, make the fried corn and peas. Melt the butter in a large frying pan (skillet). Add the frozen sweetcorn and peas and stir-fry, stirring occasionally, for about 10 minutes. Add the salt and

chilli powder and fry for a further 5 minutes.

7 Sprinkle over the lemon juice and garnish with fresh coriander (cilantro) leaves.

8 Transfer the chicken and (bell) pepper mixture to serving plates and serve with the fried corn and peas.

Chicken & Onions

Serves 4

INGREDIENTS

300 ml/½ pint/1¼ cups oil
4 medium onions, finely
    chopped
1½ tsp fresh ginger root,
    finely chopped
1½ tsp garam masala
1½ tsp fresh garlic, crushed

1 tsp chilli powder
1 tsp ground coriander
3 whole cardamoms
3 peppercorns
3 tbsp tomato purée (paste)
8 chicken thighs, skinned

300 ml/½ pint/1¼ cups
    water
2 tbsp lemon juice
1 green chilli
fresh coriander (cilantro)
    leaves
green chilli strips, to garnish

1 Heat the oil in a large frying pan (skillet). Add the onion and fry, stirring occasionally, until golden brown.

2 Reduce the heat and add the ginger, garam masala, garlic, chilli powder, ground coriander, whole cardamoms and the peppercorns, stirring well to mix.

3 Add the tomato purée (paste) to the mixture in the frying pan (skillet)

and stir-fry with the spices for 5–7 minutes.

4 Add the chicken thighs to the pan and toss in the spice mixture to coat them thoroughly

5 Pour the water into the saucepan, cover and leave the curry to simmer for 20–25 minutes.

6 Add the lemon juice, green chilli and coriander (cilantro) to the mixture, and combine.

7 Transfer the chicken and onions to warmed serving plates, garnish and serve hot.

COOK'S TIP

A dish of meat cooked with plenty of onions is called a Do Pyaza. This curry definitely improves if made in advance and then reheated before serving. This develops the flavours and makes them deeper.

Chicken Khorma

Serves 4-6

INGREDIENTS

1 1/2 tsp fresh ginger root, finely chopped
1 1/2 tsp fresh garlic, crushed
2 tsp garam masala
1 tsp chilli powder
1 tsp salt
1 tsp black cumin seeds

3 green cardamoms, with husks removed and seeds crushed
1 tsp ground coriander
1 tsp ground almonds
150 ml/5 fl oz/2/3 cup natural yogurt
8 whole chicken breasts, skinned

300 ml/1/2 pint/1 1/4 cups oil
2 medium onions, sliced
150 ml/1/4 pint/2/3 cup water
fresh coriander (cilantro) leaves
green chillies, chopped
boiled rice, to serve

1 Mix the ginger, garlic, garam masala, chilli powder, salt, black cumin seeds, green cardamoms, ground coriander and almonds with the yogurt.

2 Spoon the yogurt and spice mixture over the chicken breasts and set aside to marinate.

3 Heat the oil in a large frying pan (skillet). Add the onions to the pan and fry until a golden brown colour.

4 Add the chicken breasts to the pan, stir-frying for 5–7 minutes.

5 Add the water, cover and leave to simmer for 20–25 minutes.

6 Add the coriander (cilantro) leaves and green chillies and cook for a further 10 minutes,

stirring gently from time to time.

7 Transfer to a serving plate and serve with boiled rice.

VARIATION

Chicken portions may be used instead of breasts, if preferred, and should be cooked for 10 minutes longer in step 5.

Buttered Chicken

Serves 4-6

INGREDIENTS

100 g/3¹/₂ oz/8 tbsp unsalted
  butter
1 tbsp oil
2 medium onions, finely
  chopped
1 tsp fresh ginger root, finely
  chopped
2 tsp garam masala
2 tsp ground coriander
1 tsp chilli powder

1 tsp black cumin seeds
1 tsp fresh garlic, crushed
1 tsp salt
3 whole green cardamoms
3 whole black peppercorns
150 ml/5 fl oz/²/₃ cup natural
  yogurt
2 tbsp tomato purée (paste)
8 chicken pieces, skinned
150 ml/¹/₄ pint/²/₃ cup water

2 whole bay leaves
150 ml/5 fl oz/²/₃ cup single
  (light) cream

TO GARNISH:
fresh coriander (cilantro)
  leaves
2 green chillies, chopped

1 Heat the butter and oil in a large frying pan (skillet). Add the onions and fry until golden, stirring. Reduce the heat.

2 Crush the fresh ginger and place in a bowl. Add the garam masala, ground coriander, ginger, chilli powder, black cumin seeds, garlic, salt, cardamoms and black peppercorns and blend.

Add the yogurt and tomato purée (paste) and stir to combine.

3 Add the chicken pieces to the yogurt and spice mixture and stir them to coat well.

4 Add the chicken to the onions in the pan and stir-fry vigorously, making semi-circular movements, for 5-7 minutes.

5 Add the water and the bay leaves to the mixture in the pan and leave to simmer for 30 minutes, stirring occasionally.

6 Add the cream and cook for a further 10-15 minutes.

7 Garnish with fresh coriander (cilantro) and chillies and serve hot.

Spicy Roast Chicken

Serves 4

INGREDIENTS

50 g/1³/₄ oz/¹/₄ cup ground
    almonds
50 g/1³/₄ oz/¹/₃ cup
    desiccated (shredded)
    coconut
150 ml/¹/₄ pint/²/₃ cup oil
1 medium onion, finely
    chopped

1 tsp fresh ginger root,
    chopped
1 tsp fresh garlic, crushed
1 tsp chilli powder
1¹/₂ tsp garam masala
1 tsp salt
150 ml/5 fl oz/²/₃ cup yogurt
4 chicken quarters, skinned

green salad leaves, to serve

TO GARNISH:
fresh coriander (cilantro)
    leaves
1 lemon, cut into wedges

1 In a heavy-based
saucepan, dry roast the
ground almonds and
coconut and set aside.

2 Heat the oil in a frying
pan (skillet) and fry
the onion, stirring, until
golden brown.

3 Place the ginger, garlic,
chilli powder, garam
masala and salt in a bowl
and mix with the yogurt.
Add the almonds and
coconut and mix well.

4 Add the onions to the
spice mixture, blend
and set aside.

5 Arrange the chicken
quarters in the bottom
of a heatproof dish. Spoon
the spice mixture over the
chicken sparingly.

6 Cook in a pre-heated
oven, 160°C/425°F/Gas
Mark 3, for 35–45 minutes.
Check that the chicken is
cooked thoroughly by
piercing the thickest part of

the meat with a sharp knife
or a fine skewer – the
juices will run clear when
the chicken is cooked
through. Garnish with the
coriander (cilantro) and
lemon wedges and serve
with a salad.

COOK'S TIP

*If you want a more spicy
dish, add more chilli powder
and garam masala.*

Chicken Jalfrezi

Serves 4

INGREDIENTS

1 tsp mustard oil
3 tbsp vegetable oil
1 large onion, chopped finely
3 garlic cloves, crushed
1 tbsp tomato purée (paste)
2 tomatoes, peeled and
    chopped
1 tsp ground turmeric

$1/2$ tsp cumin seeds, ground
$1/2$ tsp coriander seeds, ground
$1/2$ tsp chilli powder
$1/2$ tsp garam masala
1 tsp red wine vinegar
1 small red (bell) pepper,
    chopped

125 g/4 oz/1 cup frozen broad
    (fava) beans
500 g/1 lb cooked chicken
    breasts, cut into bite-sized
    pieces
salt
fresh coriander (cilantro)
    sprigs, to garnish

1 Heat the mustard oil in a large, frying pan (skillet) set over a high heat for about 1 minute until it begins to smoke. Add the vegetable oil, reduce the heat and then add the onion and the garlic. Fry the garlic and onion until they are golden.

2 Add the tomato purée (paste), chopped tomatoes, ground turmeric, cumin and coriander seeds, chilli powder, garam masala and red wine vinegar to the frying pan (skillet). Stir the mixture until fragrant.

3 Add the red (bell) pepper and broad (fava) beans and stir for 2 minutes until the (bell) pepper is softened. Stir in the chicken, and salt to taste. Leave the curry to simmer gently for 6-8 minutes until the chicken is heated through and the beans are tender.

4 Serve garnished with coriander (cilantro).

COOK'S TIP

This dish is an ideal way of making use of leftover poultry – turkey, duck or quail. Any variety of beans works well, but vegetables are just as useful, especially root vegetables, courgettes (zucchini), potatoes or broccoli. Leafy vegetables will not be so successful.

Chilli Chicken

Serves 4

INGREDIENTS

350 g/12 oz skinless, boneless
    lean chicken
1/2 tsp salt
1 egg white, lightly beaten
2 tbsp cornflour (cornstarch)
4 tbsp vegetable oil
2 garlic cloves, crushed

1-cm/1/2-inch piece fresh root
    ginger, grated
1 red (bell) pepper, seeded and
    diced
1 green (bell) pepper, seeded
    and diced
2 fresh red chillies, chopped

2 tbsp light soy sauce
1 tbsp dry sherry or Chinese
    rice wine
1 tbsp wine vinegar

1 Cut the chicken into cubes and place in a mixing bowl. Add the salt, egg white, cornflour (cornstarch) and 1 tbsp of the oil. Turn the chicken in the mixture to coat well.

2 Heat the remaining oil in a preheated wok. Add the garlic and ginger and stir-fry for 30 seconds.

3 Add the chicken pieces to the wok and stir-fry for 2–3 minutes, or until browned.

4 Stir in the (bell) peppers, chillies, soy sauce, sherry or Chinese rice wine and wine vinegar and cook for 2–3 minutes, until the chicken is cooked through. Transfer to a serving dish and serve.

VARIATION

This recipe works well if you use 350 g/12 oz lean steak, cut into thin strips or 450 g/ 1 lb raw prawns (shrimp) instead of the chicken.

COOK'S TIP

When preparing chillies, wear rubber gloves to prevent the juices from burning and irritating your hands. Be careful not to touch your face, especially your lips or eyes, until you have washed your hands.

Lemon Chicken

Serves 4

INGREDIENTS

vegetable oil, for deep-frying
650 g/1 1/2 lb skinless, boneless
    chicken, cut into strips
lemon slices and shredded
    spring onions (scallions),
    to garnish

SAUCE:
1 tbsp cornflour (cornstarch)
6 tbsp cold water
3 tbsp fresh lemon juice
2 tbsp sweet sherry
1/2 tsp caster (superfine) sugar

1 Heat the oil in a wok until almost smoking. Reduce the heat and stir-fry the chicken strips for 3–4 minutes, until cooked through. Remove the chicken with a slotted spoon, set aside and keep warm. Drain the oil from the wok.

2 To make the sauce, mix the cornflour with 2 tablespoons of the water to form a paste.

3 Pour the lemon juice and remaining water into the mixture in the wok. Add the sherry and sugar and bring to the boil, stirring until the sugar has completely dissolved.

4 Stir in the cornflour mixture and return to the boil. Reduce the heat and simmer, stirring constantly, for 2–3 minutes, until the sauce is thickened and clear.

5 Transfer the chicken to a warm serving plate and pour the sauce over the top. Garnish with the lemon slices and shredded spring onions (scallions) and serve immediately.

COOK'S TIP

If you would prefer to use chicken portions rather than strips, cook them in the oil, covered, over a low heat for about 30 minutes, or until cooked through.

Braised Chicken

Serves 4

INGREDIENTS

1.5 kg/3 lb 5 oz chicken
3 tbsp vegetable oil
1 tbsp peanut oil
2 tbsp dark brown sugar
5 tbsp dark soy sauce

150 ml/^{1}/4 pint/^{2}/3 cup water
2 garlic cloves, crushed
1 small onion, chopped
1 fresh red chilli, chopped

celery leaves and chives, to
garnish

1 Clean the chicken with damp kitchen paper (paper towels).

2 Put the oil in a wok, add the sugar and heat gently until the sugar caramelizes. Stir in the soy sauce. Add the chicken and turn it in the mixture to coat on all sides.

3 Add the water, garlic, onion and chilli. Cover and simmer, turning chicken occasionally, for 1 hour, or until cooked through. Test by piercing a thigh with the point of a

knife or a skewer – the juices will run clear when the chicken is cooked.

4 Remove the chicken from the wok and transfer to a serving plate. Increase the heat and reduce the sauce in the wok until thickened. Garnish the chicken and serve with the sauce.

COOK'S TIP

When caramelizing the sugar, do not turn the heat too high, or it may burn.

VARIATION

For a spicier sauce, add 1 tbsp finely chopped fresh root ginger and 1 tbsp ground Szechuan peppercorns with the chilli in step 3. If the flavour of dark soy sauce is too strong for your taste, substitute 2 tbsp dark soy sauce and 3 tbsp light soy sauce. This will result in a more delicate taste without sacrificing the attractive colour of the dish.

Chicken With Cashew Nuts & Vegetables

Serves 4

INGREDIENTS

300 g/10 1/2 oz boneless,
skinless chicken breasts
1 tbsp cornflour (cornstarch)
1 tsp sesame oil
1 tbsp hoisin sauce
1 tsp light soy sauce
3 garlic cloves, crushed
2 tbsp vegetable oil

75 g/2 3/4 oz/3/4 cup unsalted
cashew nuts
25 g/1 oz mangetout (snow
peas)
1 celery stick, sliced
1 onion, cut into 8 pieces
60 g/2 oz beansprouts

1 red (bell) pepper, seeded and
diced

SAUCE:
2 tsp cornflour (cornstarch)
2 tbsp hoisin sauce
200 ml/7 fl oz/7/8 cup chicken
stock

1 Trim any fat from the chicken breasts and cut the meat into thin strips. Place the chicken in a large bowl. Sprinkle with the cornflour (cornstarch) and toss to coat the chicken strips in it, shaking off any excess. Mix together the sesame oil, hoisin sauce, soy sauce and 1 garlic clove. Pour this mixture over the chicken, turning to coat. Marinate for 20 minutes.

2 Heat half of the vegetable oil in a preheated wok. Add the cashew nuts and stir-fry for 1 minute, until browned. Add the mangetout (snow peas), celery, the remaining garlic, the onion, bean-sprouts and red (bell) pepper and cook, stirring occasionally, for 2–3 minutes. Remove the vegetables from the wok with a slotted spoon, set aside and keep warm.

3 Heat the remaining oil in the wok. Remove the chicken from the marinade and stir-fry for 3–4 minutes. Return the vegetables to the wok.

4 To make the sauce, mix the cornflour (cornstarch), hoisin sauce and chicken stock and pour into the wok. Bring to the boil, stirring until thickened and clear. Serve.

Chicken with Yellow Bean Sauce

Serves 4

INGREDIENTS

450 g/1 lb skinless, boneless
   chicken breasts
1 egg white, beaten
1 tbsp cornflour (cornstarch)
1 tbsp rice wine vinegar
1 tbsp light soy sauce

1 tsp caster (superfine) sugar
3 tbsp vegetable oil
1 garlic clove, crushed
1-cm/^{1}/2-inch piece fresh root
   ginger, grated

1 green (bell) pepper, seeded
   and diced
2 large mushrooms, sliced
3 tbsp yellow bean sauce
yellow or green (bell) pepper
   strips, to garnish

1 Trim any fat from the chicken. Cut the meat into 2.5-cm/1-inch cubes.

2 Mix the egg white and cornflour (cornstarch) in a shallow bowl. Add the chicken and turn in the mixture to coat. Set aside for 20 minutes.

3 Mix the vinegar, soy sauce and sugar in a bowl.

4 Remove the chicken from the egg white mixture.

5 Heat the oil in a preheated wok, add the chicken and stir-fry for 3–4 minutes, until golden brown. Remove the chicken from the wok with a slotted spoon, set aside and keep warm.

6 Add the garlic, ginger, (bell) pepper and mushrooms to the wok and stir-fry for 1–2 minutes.

7 Add the yellow bean sauce and cook for 1 minute. Stir in the vinegar mixture and return

the chicken to the wok. Cook for 1–2 minutes and serve hot, garnished with (bell) pepper strips.

VARIATION

Black bean sauce would work equally well with this recipe. Although this would affect the appearance of the dish, as it is much darker in colour, the flavours would be compatible.

Spicy Peanut Chicken

Serves 4

INGREDIENTS

300 g/10¹/₂ oz skinless,
   boneless chicken breast
2 tbsp peanut oil
125 g/4¹/₂ oz/1 cup shelled
   peanuts
1 fresh red chilli, sliced
1 green (bell) pepper, seeded
   and cut into strips

1 tsp sesame oil
fried rice, to serve

SAUCE:
150 ml/¹/₄ pint/²/₃ cup
   chicken stock
1 tbsp Chinese rice wine or
   dry sherry

1 tbsp light soy sauce
1¹/₂ tsp light brown sugar
2 garlic cloves, crushed
1 tsp grated fresh root ginger
1 tsp rice wine vinegar

1 Trim any fat from the chicken and cut the meat into 2.5-cm/1-inch cubes. Set aside.

2 Heat the peanut oil in a preheated wok. Add the peanuts and stir-fry for 1 minute. Remove the peanuts with a slotted spoon and set aside.

3 Add the chicken to the wok and cook for 1–2 minutes. Stir in the chilli and (bell) pepper and cook

for 1 minute. Remove from the wok with a slotted spoon.

4 Put half of the peanuts in a food processor and process until almost smooth. Alternatively, place them in a plastic bag and crush with a rolling pin.

5 To make the sauce, add the chicken stock, Chinese rice wine or dry sherry, soy sauce, sugar, garlic, ginger and rice wine vinegar to the wok.

6 Heat the sauce without boiling and stir in the peanut purée, remaining peanuts, chicken, chilli and (bell) pepper. Sprinkle with the sesame oil, stir and cook for 1 minute. Serve hot.

COOK'S TIP

If necessary, process the peanuts with a little of the stock in step 4 to form a softer paste.

Chinese Chicken Salad

Serves 4

225 g/8 oz skinless, boneless
    chicken breasts
2 tsp light soy sauce
1 tsp sesame oil
1 tsp sesame seeds
2 tbsp vegetable oil
125 g/4^1/$_2$ oz beansprouts

1 red (bell) pepper, seeded and
    thinly sliced
1 carrot, cut into matchsticks
3 baby corn cobs, sliced
snipped chives and carrot
    matchsticks, to garnish

SAUCE:
2 tsp rice wine vinegar
1 tbsp light soy sauce
dash of chilli oil

1 Place the chicken in a shallow glass dish.

2 Mix together the soy sauce and sesame oil and pour over the chicken. Sprinkle with sesame seeds and leave to stand for 20 minutes.

3 Remove the chicken from the marinade and cut the meat into slices.

4 Heat the oil in a preheated wok. Add the chicken and fry for 4–5 minutes, until cooked through and golden brown on both sides. Remove the chicken from the wok with a slotted spoon, set aside and leave to cool.

5 Add the beansprouts, (bell) pepper, carrot and baby corn cobs to the wok and stir-fry for 2–3 minutes. Remove from the wok with a slotted spoon, set aside and leave to cool.

6 To make the sauce, mix the rice wine vinegar, light soy sauce and chilli oil together.

7 Arrange the chicken and vegetables on a serving plate. Spoon the sauce over the salad, garnish and serve.

COOK'S TIP

If you have time, make the sauce and leave to stand for 30 minutes for the flavours to fully develop.

Wholemeal (Whole wheat) Spaghetti with Suprêmes of Chicken Nell Gwyn

Serves 4

INGREDIENTS
---

25 ml/1 fl oz/$\frac{1}{8}$ cup rapeseed oil

3 tbsp olive oil

4 x 225 g/8 oz chicken suprêmes

150 ml/$\frac{1}{4}$ pint/$\frac{5}{8}$ cup orange brandy

15 g/$\frac{1}{2}$ oz/2 tbsp plain (all purpose) flour

150 ml/$\frac{1}{4}$ pint/$\frac{5}{8}$ cup freshly squeezed orange juice

25 g/1 oz courgette (zucchini), cut into matchstick strips

25 g/1 oz red (bell) pepper, cut into matchstick strips

25 g/1 oz leek, finely shredded

400 g/14 oz dried wholemeal (whole wheat) spaghetti

3 large oranges, peeled and cut into segments

rind of 1 orange, cut into very fine strips

2 tbsp chopped fresh tarragon

150 ml/$\frac{1}{4}$ pint/$\frac{5}{8}$ cup fromage frais or ricotta cheese

salt and pepper

---

1 Heat the rapeseed oil and 1 tbsp of the olive oil in a frying pan (skillet). Add the chicken and cook quickly until golden brown. Add the orange brandy and cook for 3 minutes. Sprinkle over the flour and cook for 2 minutes.

2 Lower the heat and add the orange juice, courgette (zucchini), (bell) pepper and leek and season. Simmer for 5 minutes until the sauce has thickened.

3 Meanwhile, bring a pan of salted water to the boil. Add the spaghetti and 1 tbsp of the olive oil and cook for 10 minutes. Drain, transfer to a serving dish and drizzle over the remaining oil.

4 Add half the orange segments, half the orange rind, the tarragon and fromage frais or ricotta cheese to the sauce in the pan and cook for 3 minutes.

5 Place the chicken on top of the pasta, pour over a little sauce, garnish with orange segments and rind. Serve immediately.

Chicken & Wild Mushroom Lasagne

Serves 4

INGREDIENTS

butter, for greasing
14 sheets pre-cooked lasagne
850 ml/$1^1/_2$ pints/$3^3/_4$ cups
  Béchamel Sauce
75 g/3 oz/1 cup grated
  Parmesan cheese

CHICKEN & WILD MUSHROOM
  SAUCE:
2 tbsp olive oil
2 garlic cloves, crushed
1 large onion, finely chopped
225 g/8 oz wild mushrooms,
  sliced
300 g/$10^1/_2$ oz/$2^1/_2$ cups
  minced (ground) chicken
80 g/3 oz chicken livers,
  finely chopped

115 g/4 oz Parma ham
  (prosciutto), diced
150 ml/$^1/_4$ pint/$^5/_8$ cup
  Marsala
285 g/10 oz can chopped
  tomatoes
1 tbsp chopped fresh basil
  leaves
2 tbsp tomato purée (paste)
salt and pepper

1 To make the sauce, heat the olive oil in a large saucepan. Add the garlic, onion and mushrooms and cook for 6 minutes.

2 Add the minced (ground) chicken, chicken livers and Parma ham (prosciutto) and cook for 12 minutes, until the meat has browned.

3 Stir the Marsala, tomatoes, basil and tomato purée (paste) into the pan and cook for 4 minutes. Season, cover and simmer for 30 minutes. Stir and simmer for a further 15 minutes.

4 Arrange the lasagne over the base of a greased ovenproof dish, spoon over a layer of

chicken and wild mushroom sauce, then a layer of Béchamel Sauce. Place another layer of lasagne on top and repeat the process twice, finishing with a layer of Béchamel Sauce. Sprinkle over the grated cheese and bake in a preheated oven at 190°C/375°F/Gas 5 for 35 minutes until golden brown. Serve immediately.

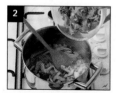

Mustard Baked Chicken with Pasta Shells

Serves 4

INGREDIENTS

8 chicken pieces
(about 115 g/4 oz each)
60g/2 oz/4 tbsp butter, melted
4 tbsp mild mustard (see
Cook's Tip)

2 tbsp lemon juice
1 tbsp brown sugar
1 tsp paprika
3 tbsp poppy seeds
400 g/14 oz fresh pasta shells

1 tbsp olive oil
salt and pepper

1 Arrange the chicken, smooth side down, in an ovenproof dish.

2 Combine the butter, mustard, lemon juice, sugar, paprika and salt and pepper. Brush the mixture over the upper surfaces of the chicken pieces and bake in a preheated oven at 200°C/400°F/Gas 6 for 15 minutes.

3 Remove the dish from the oven and turn over the chicken pieces. Coat the upper surfaces of the chicken with the remaining mustard mixture, sprinkle with poppy seeds and return to the oven for a further 15 minutes.

4 Meanwhile, bring a large pan of lightly salted water to the boil. Add the pasta shells and olive oil and cook until tender, but still firm to the bite.

5 Drain the pasta and arrange on a warmed serving dish. Top with the chicken, pour over the sauce and serve immediately.

COOK'S TIP

Dijon is the type of mustard most often used in cooking, as it has a clean and only mildly spicy flavour. German mustard has a sweet-sour taste, with Bavarian mustard being slightly sweeter. American mustard is mild and sweet.

Chicken Suprêmes Filled with Tiger Prawns (Shrimp) on a Bed of Pasta

Serves 4

INGREDIENTS

4 x 200 g/7 oz chicken
  suprêmes, trimmed
115 g/4 oz large spinach leaves,
  trimmed and blanched in
  hot salted water
4 slices of Parma ham
  (prosciutto)

12–16 raw tiger prawns
  (shrimp), shelled and
  deveined
450g/1 lb dried tagliatelle
1 tbsp olive oil
60 g/2 oz/4 tbsp butter, plus
  extra for greasing

3 leeks, shredded
1 large carrot, grated
150 ml/^{1}/4 pint/^{5}/8 cup
  thick mayonnaise
2 large cooked beetroot (beet)
salt

1 Place each suprême between 2 pieces of baking parchment and pound to flatten.

2 Divide half the spinach between the suprêmes, add a slice of ham to each and top with spinach. Place 3–4 prawns (shrimp) on top. Roll up each suprême to form a parcel. Wrap each parcel in greased foil, place on a baking (cookie) sheet and bake in a preheated oven at 200°C/400°F/Gas 6 for 20 minutes.

3 Cook the pasta with the oil in salted boiling water until tender. Drain and transfer to a warm dish.

4 Melt the butter and fry the leeks and carrot for 3 minutes. Transfer to the centre of the pasta.

5 Work the mayonnaise and 1 beetroot (beet) in a food processor until smooth. Rub through a strainer and pour around the pasta and vegetables.

6 Cut the remaining beetroot (beet) into diamond shapes and place them around the mayonnaise. Remove the foil from the chicken and cut the suprêmes into thin slices. Arrange the slices on top of the vegetables and pasta, and serve.

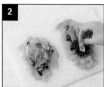

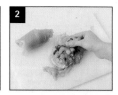

Favourite Barbecued (Grilled) Chicken

Serves 4

INGREDIENTS
---

8 chicken wings or 1 chicken
   cut into 8 portions
3 tbsp tomato purée (paste)

3 tbsp brown fruity sauce
1 tbsp white wine vinegar
1 tbsp clear honey

1 tbsp olive oil
1 clove garlic, crushed
   (optional)
salad leaves, to serve

---

1 Remove the skin from the chicken if you want to reduce the fat in the dish.

2 To make the barbecue glaze, place the tomato purée (paste), brown fruity sauce, white wine vinegar, honey, oil and garlic in a small bowl. Stir all of the ingredients together until they are thoroughly blended.

3 Brush the barbecue (grill) glaze over the chicken and barbecue

(grill) over hot coals for 15–20 minutes. Turn the chicken portions over occasionally and baste frequently with the barbecue (grill) glaze. If the chicken begins to blacken before it is cooked, raise the rack if possible or move the chicken to a cooler part of the barbecue (grill) to slow down the cooking.

4 Transfer the barbecued (grilled) chicken to warm serving plates and serve with a selection of fresh salad leaves.

VARIATION

This barbecue (grill) glaze also makes a very good baste to brush over pork chops.

COOK'S TIP

When poultry is cooked over a very hot barbecue (grill) the heat immediately seals in all of the juices, leaving the meat succulent. For this reason you must make sure that the coals are hot enough before starting to barbecue (grill).

Sticky Chicken Drumsticks

Serves 10

INGREDIENTS

10 chicken drumsticks
4 tbsp fine-cut orange
   marmalade

1 tbsp Worcestershire sauce
grated rind and juice of
   $\frac{1}{2}$ orange
salt and pepper

TO SERVE:
cherry tomatoes
salad leaves

1 Using a sharp knife, make 2–3 slashes in the flesh of each chicken drumstick.

2 Bring a large saucepan of water to the boil and add the chicken drumsticks. Cover the pan, return to the boil and cook for 5–10 minutes. Remove the chicken and drain thoroughly.

3 Meanwhile, make the baste. Place the orange marmalade, Worcestershire sauce, orange rind and juice and salt and pepper to taste in a small saucepan.

Heat gently, stirring continuously, until the marmalade melts and all of the ingredients are well combined.

4 Brush the baste over the par-cooked chicken drumsticks and transfer them to the barbecue (grill) to complete cooking. Barbecue (grill) over hot coals for about 10 minutes, turning and basting frequently with the remaining baste.

5 Carefully thread 3 cherry tomatoes on to a skewer and transfer to

the barbecue (grill) for 1–2 minutes.

6 Transfer the chicken drumsticks to serving plates. Serve with the cherry tomato skewers and a selection of fresh salad leaves.

COOK'S TIP

Par-cooking the chicken is an ideal way of making sure that it is cooked through without becoming overcooked and burned on the outside.

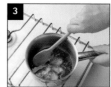

Sweet Maple Chicken

Serves 6

INGREDIENTS

2 boned chicken thighs
5 tbsp maple syrup
1 tbsp caster (superfine) sugar
grated rind and juice of
 $^1/_2$ orange
2 tbsp tomato ketchup

2 tsp Worcestershire sauce

TO GARNISH:
slices of orange
sprig of flat-leaf parsley

TO SERVE:
focaccia bread
salad leaves
cherry tomatoes, quartered

1 Using a sharp knife, make 2–3 slashes in the flesh of the chicken. Place the chicken in a shallow, non-metallic dish.

2 To make the marinade, mix together the maple syrup, sugar, orange rind and juice, ketchup and Worcestershire sauce.

3 Pour the marinade over the chicken, tossing the chicken to coat thoroughly. Cover and leave to chill in the refrigerator until required.

4 Remove the chicken from the marinade, reserving the marinade for basting.

5 Transfer the chicken to the barbecue (grill) and cook over hot coals for 20 minutes, turning and basting with the marinade.

6 Transfer the chicken to serving plates and garnish with slices of orange and a sprig of fresh-leaf parsley. Serve with focaccia bread, fresh salad leaves and cherry tomatoes.

COOK'S TIP

If time is short you can omit the marinating time. If you use chicken quarters, rather than the smaller thigh portions, par-boil them for 10 minutes before brushing with the marinade and barbecueing (grilling).

Chicken Satay

Serves 4

INGREDIENTS

2 chicken breasts, skinned and boned

MARINADE:
4 tbsp sunflower oil
2 cloves garlic, crushed
3 tbsp fresh, chopped coriander (cilantro)
1 tbsp caster (superfine) sugar

$^1/_2$ tsp ground cumin
$^1/_2$ tsp ground coriander
1 tbsp soy sauce
1 red or green chilli, deseeded
salt and pepper

SAUCE:
2 tbsp sunflower oil
1 small onion, chopped finely

1 red or green chilli, deseeded and chopped
$^1/_2$ tsp ground coriander
$^1/_2$ tsp ground cumin
8 tbsp peanut butter
8 tbsp chicken stock or water
1 tbsp block coconut

1 Soak 8 wooden skewers in a large, shallow dish of cold water for at least 30 minutes. This will prevent the skewers from burning on the hot grill.

2 Cut the chicken lengthwise into 8 long strips. Thread the strips of chicken, concertina-style, on to the skewers and set them aside while you make the marinade.

3 Place the ingredients for the marinade in a food processor and process until smooth.

4 Coat the chicken with the marinade paste, cover and leave to chill in the refrigerator for at least 2 hours.

5 To make the sauce, heat the oil in a small pan and fry the onion and chilli until they are softened but not browned. Stir in the spices and cook for 1 minute. Add the remaining sauce ingredients and cook the mixture gently for 5 minutes. Keep warm.

6 Barbecue (grill) the chicken skewers over hot coals for about 10 minutes, basting with any remaining marinade. Serve immediately with the warm sauce.

Thai-style Chicken Skewers

Serves 4

INGREDIENTS

4 chicken breasts, skinned and
    boned
1 onion, peeled and cut into
    wedges
1 large red (bell) pepper,
    deseeded

1 large yellow (bell) pepper
    deseeded
12 kaffir lime leaves
2 tbsp sunflower oil
2 tbsp lime juice
tomato halves, to serve

MARINADE:
1 tbsp Thai red curry paste
150 ml/5 fl oz/²/3 cup canned
    coconut milk

1 To make the marinade, place the red curry paste in a small saucepan over a medium heat and cook for 1 minute. Add half of the coconut milk to the saucepan and bring the mixture to the boil. Boil gently for 2–3 minutes until the liquid has reduced by about two-thirds.

2 Remove the saucepan from the heat and stir in the remaining coconut milk. Set the mixture aside to cool.

3 Cut the chicken into 2.5 cm/1 inch pieces. Stir the chicken into the cold marinade, cover and leave to chill for at least 2 hours.

4 Cut the onion into wedges and the (bell) peppers into 2.5 cm/1 inch pieces.

5 Remove the chicken pieces from the marinade and thread them on to skewers, alternating the chicken with the vegetables and lime leaves.

6 Combine the oil and lime juice in a small bowl and brush the mixture over the kebabs (kabobs). Barbecue (grill) the skewers over hot coals, turning and basting for 10–15 minutes until the chicken is cooked through. Barbecue (grill) the tomato halves and serve with the chicken skewers.

Sesame Chicken Brochettes with Cranberry Sauce

Makes 8

INGREDIENTS

4 chicken breasts, skinned and
    boned
4 tbsp dry white wine
1 tbsp light muscovado sugar
2 tbsp sunflower oil
100 g/3^1/$_2$ oz sesame seeds

salt and pepper

TO SERVE:
boiled new potatoes
green salad leaves

SAUCE:
175 g/6 oz cranberries
150 ml/5 fl oz/^{2}/$_3$ cup
    cranberry juice drink
2 tbsp light muscovado sugar

1 Cut the chicken into 2.5 cm/1 inch pieces. Put the wine, sugar, oil and salt and pepper to taste in a large bowl, stirring to combine. Add the chicken pieces and toss to coat. Leave to marinate for at least 30 minutes, turning the chicken occasionally.

2 To make the sauce, place the ingredients in a small saucepan and bring slowly to the boil, stirring. Simmer gently for

5–10 minutes until the cranberries are soft and pulpy. Taste and add a little extra sugar if wished. Keep warm or leave to chill.

3 Remove the chicken pieces from the marinade with a perforated spoon. Thread the chicken pieces on to 8 skewers, spacing them slightly apart to ensure even cooking.

4 Barbecue (grill) on an oiled rack over hot

coals for 4–5 minutes on each side until just cooked. Brush several times with the marinade.

5 Remove the chicken skewers from the rack and roll in the sesame seeds. Return to the barbecue (grill) and cook for about 1 minute on each side or until the sesame seeds are toasted. Serve with the cranberry sauce, new potatoes and green salad leaves.

Chicken Skewers with Red (Bell) Pepper Sauce

Serves 4

INGREDIENTS

3 chicken breasts, skinned and boned
6 tbsp olive oil
4 tbsp lemon juice
$1/2$ small onion, grated
1 tbsp fresh, chopped sage
8 tbsp sage and onion stuffing mix

6 tbsp boiling water
2 green (bell) peppers, deseeded

SAUCE:
1 tbsp olive oil
1 red (bell) pepper, deseeded and chopped finely

1 small onion, chopped finely
pinch sugar
210 g/$7^1/2$ oz can chopped tomatoes

1 Cut the chicken into evenly sized pieces. Mix the oil, lemon juice, grated onion and sage and pour into a polythene bag. Add the chicken, seal and shake. Marinate for 30 minutes, shaking occasionally. Place the stuffing mix in a bowl and add the boiling water, stirring well.

2 Cut each (bell) pepper into 6 strips, then blanch in boiling water for 3–4 minutes. Drain and refresh under running water, then drain again.

3 Form about 1 tsp of the stuffing mixture into a ball and roll it up in a strip of (bell) pepper. Repeat for the remaining stuffing mixture and (bell) pepper strips. Thread 3 rolls on to each skewer alternately with pieces of chicken. Chill.

4 To make the sauce, heat the oil in a small pan and fry the (bell) pepper and onion for 5 minutes. Add the sugar and tomatoes and simmer for 5 minutes. Set aside and keep warm.

5 Barbecue (grill) the skewers on an oiled rack over hot coals, basting frequently, for 15 minutes. Serve with the sauce.

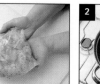

Chicken Skewers with Lemon & Coriander (Cilantro)

Serves 4

INGREDIENTS

4 chicken breasts, skinned and
   boned
1 tsp ground coriander
2 tsp lemon juice

300 ml/^{1}/$_2$ pint/1^1/$_4$ cups
   natural yogurt
1 lemon

2 tbsp chopped, fresh
   coriander (cilantro)
oil for brushing
salt and pepper

1 Cut the chicken into
2.5 cm/1 inch pieces
and place them in a
shallow, non-metallic dish.

2 Add the coriander,
lemon juice, salt and
pepper to taste and 4 tbsp
of the yogurt to the
chicken and mix together
until thoroughly
combined. Cover and leave
to chill for at least 2 hours,
preferably overnight.

3 To make the lemon
yogurt, peel and finely
chop the lemon, discarding

any pips. Stir the lemon
into the yogurt, with the
fresh coriander (cilantro).
Chill in the refrigerator.

4 Thread the chicken
pieces on to skewers.
Brush the rack with oil and
barbecue (grill) over hot
coals for about 15 minutes,
basting with the oil.

5 Transfer the kebabs
(kabobs) to warm
serving plates and garnish
with coriander (cilantro),
lemon wedges and salad
leaves. Serve with yogurt.

VARIATION

*These kebabs (kabobs) are
delicious served on a bed of
blanched spinach, which has
been seasoned with salt,
pepper and nutmeg.*

COOK'S TIP

*Prepare the chicken the day
before it is needed so that it
can marinate overnight.*

Maryland Chicken Kebabs (Kabobs)

Makes 4

INGREDIENTS

8 chicken thighs, skinned and
   boned
1 tbsp white wine vinegar
1 tbsp lemon juice, plus extra
   for brushing
1 tbsp golden syrup or honey

6 tbsp olive oil
1 clove garlic, crushed
4 rashers rindless, smoked,
   streaky bacon
2 bananas
salt and pepper

TO SERVE:
4 cooked corn-on-the-cobs
mango chutney (relish)

1 Cut the chicken into bite-size pieces. Combine the vinegar, lemon juice, syrup or honey, oil, garlic and salt and pepper to taste in a large bowl. Add the chicken to the marinade and toss until well coated. Cover and leave to marinate for 1–2 hours.

2 Stretch the bacon rashers with the back of a knife and then cut each bacon rasher in half. Cut the bananas into 2.5 cm/ 1 inch lengths and brush them with lemon juice to prevent any discoloration.

3 Wrap a piece of bacon around each piece of banana.

4 Remove the chicken from the marinade, reserving the marinade for basting. Thread the chicken pieces and the bacon and banana rolls alternately on to skewers.

5 Barbecue (grill) the kebabs (kabobs) over hot coals for 8–10 minutes until the chicken is completely cooked. Baste the kebabs (kabobs) with the marinade and turn the skewers frequently. Serve with corn-on-the-cobs and mango chutney (relish).

VARIATION

For a quick Maryland-style dish, omit the marinating time and cook the chicken thighs over hot coals for about 20 minutes, basting with the marinade.

This is a Parragon Book
First published in 2000
Parragon
Queen Street House
4 Queen Street
Bath BA1 1HE, UK

ISBN: 0-75253-370-3

Printed in China

Note

Cup measurements in this book are for American cups. Tablespoons are assumed to be
15 ml. Unless otherwise stated, milk is assumed to be full fat, eggs are medium and
pepper is freshly ground black pepper.